Mountain Biking in Kentucky

By
Stuart Ulferts
and
Bruce Montana

RSH Media
Louisville, Kentucky

Mountain Biking in Kentucky

By Stuart Ulferts and Bruce Montana

Published by:
RSH Media
Post Office Box 17522
Louisville, KY 40217-0522

Printed in the United States of America.

Publisher's Cataloging in Publication Data
       Ulferts, Stewart G. W., 1963 -
       Mountain Biking in Kentucky / Stewart G. W. Ulferts and
           Bruce Montana
       Includes index.
       ISBN 1-887187-04-9 (softcover)
       1. All Terrain Cycling-Kentucky-Guidebooks
       2. Kentucky-Guidebooks
       I. Montana, Bruce 1950- II. Title
       796.64097 ULF   1995
       Library of Congress Catalog Card Number: 95-68798

Contents

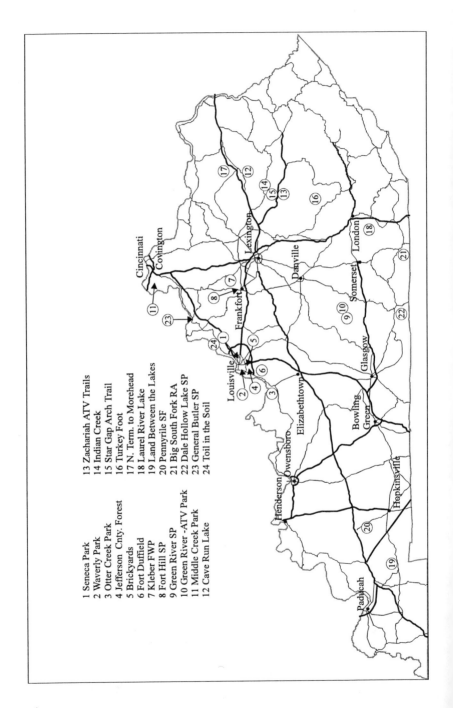

1 Seneca Park
2 Waverly Park
3 Otter Creek Park
4 Jefferson Cnty. Forest
5 Brickyards
6 Fort Duffield
7 Kleber FWP
8 Fort Hill SP
9 Green River SP
10 Green River -ATV Park
11 Middle Creek Park
12 Cave Run Lake

13 Zachariah ATV Trails
14 Indian Creek
15 Star Gap Arch Trail
16 Turkey Foot
17 N. Term. to Morehead
18 Laurel River Lake
19 Land Between the Lakes
20 Pennyrile SF
21 Big South Fork RA
22 Dale Hollow Lake SP
23 General Butler SP
24 Toil in the Soil

READ THIS FIRST !

MOUNTAIN BIKING CAN BE A DANGEROUS SPORT.
NO ONE CONNECTED TO THIS WORK IN ANY WAY
ASSUMES ANY LIABILITY FOR YOUR ACTIONS OR
ANYONE ELSE'S ACTIONS, WHETHER THEY WERE
NEGLIGENT OR NOT.

There, we've said it, now let us explain. Off road bicycling
does not have to be more risky than other outdoor activities,
but it can be dangerous if done in certain reckless ways.
Accidents and injuries make life more difficult for everyone
who enjoys off road cycling, so it's up to you to be
responsible and alert.

Follow the simple rules of the off road cyclist:

1. Ride carefully and considerately of all other users who
may be on the trail, including horses, and people who you
cannot see but who might be just around the bend.

2. Use good sense about when to ride a particular trail. Any
use of a trail, including hiking, causes erosion, but don't ride
when it is too wet or in a way that might cause undue trail
damage. Do not skid your tires, especially on a down hill.

3. Don't leave your energy bar wrapper or your punctured
inner tube on the trail. Don't hoot or holler, or act stupid.

Other people have a right to peacefully enjoy their wilderness experience too.

4. Plan your trip according to the weather and terrain and try not to get lost or injured in the middle of the woods. Doing so ruins other peoples days as well as your own.

5. Be prepared to help maintain the trails you ride on, pick up other peoples trash and do other good deeds that will enable you to ride there again. Join the local bike club that is involved in keeping trails open.

By following these rules we think you will be able to better enjoy and appreciate this fabulous sport. We know that others will be better able to appreciate us!

A final warning. Many of the trails described in this book are in hilly, isolated areas. Amenities such as drinking water, first aid, and bike repair may be many miles away. An empty water bottle, a flat tire, or a body sprain may not be any big deal when you are in your local park, close to civilization. Any of those things can be life threatening when you are ten miles from the nearest road!

Acknowledgments

We wish to acknowledge the following:

All the members of the Kentucky Mountain Bike Association who are organized state-wide to provide all Kentuckians with an off road bicycle experience.

Rocky Crady and Richard Mathews, who are two mountain bike "old timers" and have done more for the sport that many people will ever realize.

John Rowe, former director of Otter Creek Park, and the staff of Otter Creek Park, the cradle of civilization for Louisville trail bikers, who welcomed us to ride there a long time ago.

Joe Cross, who we don't know, but who developed The Big South Fork trails.

The good people down at Land Between the Lakes (PAMBA) who have added another quality racing venue to our state.

Metro Parks in Louisville, who don't know what to do with us and don't understand the off road bicycle revolution, but have at least made some efforts to listen.

The hundreds of volunteers who have made trails for everyone.

How to Use This Book

The authors are from Louisville, and admit to an unavoidable geographic bias in their reporting. Sorry, but that is life. We have been to the areas closer to Louisville more often than we have been to the areas further away; therefore, we will be able to provide more information about the closer areas. We have worked hard to provide your with the most accurate information available to us.

We are unable to describe every good trail in Kentucky because there are so many! Our goal is to give you, the reader, an overview of the most popular ones. The trail system in Kentucky is in development and new trails are constantly being built by dedicated volunteers. No one gets paid to do this but they are doing it everywhere. Thus, you should look for a new edition of this book to come out within a year or two.

Trails are by definition subject to change. Authorities may close trails to bicycles, and this happens everywhere with alarming frequency. Trails can be altered on purpose for various reasons, or be wiped out by tornadoes or mud slides (really). There is no warranty in this book that the trails we provide will always exist as we now know them. Try to get up to date information before leaving home. The best rides are invariably the ones where you discover new trails, so be flexible. We are providing this publication to help you get started, do not limit yourself.

Wherever possible we have provided contact points to enable you to call ahead. Be courteous when you do so and realize that no one is profiting by giving you free information, and in fact, they are taking time out of their day when they do. If you call a store for information and they provide it to you, patronize that store when you pass by. If you cannot get any information, try the Kentucky Mountain Bike Association Ride Hot line, which is provided in the appendix under Louisville Chapter of the Kentucky Mountain Bike Association.

This book is divided into fairly arbitrary chapters, representing perceived regions of riding areas. We have not attempted to be scientific in our divisions, Sheltowee Trace trails might just as well been included in some of the geographical chapters, such as southeastern Kentucky. We divided it up as we see it.

Each chapter has a short introduction where we listed some of the more important points of information about the region described in the chapter. Each area is then further divided by trails and trail systems, again with a short introduction.

We have provided travel directions by car from the nearest interstate. You may wish to check our directions on a road map to ensure they provide the most efficient route for you. Some directions are a toss up on which way is the quickest route. We have made the assumption that you desire the shortest and not necessarily the most scenic way. A map may help pick a more interesting route if you have time.

In our trail description, we have aspired to be concise; however, we realize the inherent limitations of written directions and we have tried to include some obvious landmarks when they do not run the risk of adding rather than reducing confusion. You may photocopy the maps and the directions for your own personal use and we encourage you to do so for use on the trail. Even more encouraged is the good idea of obtaining a topographic map from a ranger station or bookstore of the area you intend to ride. These large scale maps can be much more helpful than anything we could possibly provide in this book.

We conclude each section with notes on the conditions and surroundings, as well as any historical interest in the area that we can share.

Introduction

Kentucky is perfectly suited by location, topography and climate, for the development of off road cycling. It is inevitable that we will witness the sport's rapid growth in popularity here, as it has already spread throughout the rest of the country. Up until now there has been very little written about bike trails in our Commonwealth, yet there is obviously a need for trail information. In the foreseeable future we are only going to see more and more off road bikers in Kentucky.

This is a good thing, notwithstanding the silly controversies which have arisen between some hikers and mountain bike activists.

There has been some resentment toward bicyclists by hikers who would rather have the natural public areas all to themselves. Mountain bikers, like hikers, enjoy the outdoors, and want to have plenty of places to engage in their activities. Increased recreational use of public lands makes it less likely that government bureaucrats will decide to use the land for something else. By tolerating each other, bikers and hikers can better asure the continued preservation of the public lands they use.

Although it is the fastest growing participatory sport in the nation, a certain mystique remains around off road cycling. The youth, vigor and daring embodied by it make the sport a popular target for mass marketers who do not fully understand it. TV, ESPN and commercials all show that thrill seeking side, which is just one of many facets of the sport.

Most off road cyclists engage in the passive form of the recreation, whereby they experience nature, the outdoors, and quietude, while receiving all the benefits of vigorous exercise. These riders are content to roll along at their own pace with nothing to prove to the cameras or the crowds.

The popular name, "mountain biking," is often not accurate, and adds to misunderstanding about the sport. Off road cycling is popular in Houston, Texas; Paducah, Kentucky; Ocala, Florida, and many other places where the terrain is anything but mountainous. The association with mountains adds panache but makes the sport seem intimidating to the uninitiated flat lander.

To tell someone that you mountain bike evokes images of far away places and of "Mountain Dew" commercials. Tell the same person that you ride bicycles on dirt trails and they might well hearken back in their imagination to their childhood, and of riding their one-speed balloon tired special through the grass.

Another issue that creates misunderstanding between the experienced trail biker and the general public is location of the trails. It is to the perceived scarcity of venues to which the average person might respond, "Gee it looks fun but I don't know where to do it." There are really plenty of accessible trails in Kentucky, they just aren't that well known to all of our potential mountain bike enthusiasts out there. For them, we have written this book.

Louisville Metro Area

Louisville is an undiscovered secret of Midwestern mountain biking. There are miles of good singletrack within an hour's drive of the city limits. The multitude of venues helps keep crowding down in any one area, raising the quality of the experience. Most of these trails are in parks that are operated by the Louisville and Jefferson County Metro Parks Department. Waverly and Otter Creek Parks are the most popular destinations but each area offers unique trail conditions.

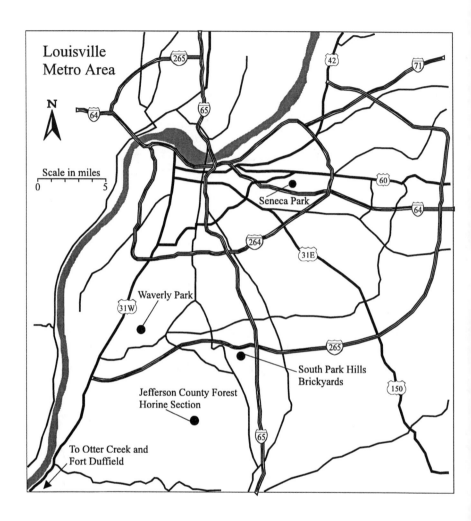

Seneca Park

Rating: Moderate Difficulty.

Trails: Wilderness Trail 3 miles.

Overview: Short but challenging urban singletrack escape within the city limits. Some paved sections, and with a couple of climbs of a few hundred yards. Watch out for horses which share this busy park with other users!

Getting There: Take Cannons Lane North off 1-64 just east of downtown Louisville. At 4-way stop, turn Left and park vehicle on Seneca Park loop.

Trail Description: Look for trailhead on Right, across street from tennis courts. Beware of road crossing 1/16 mile down trail. Cross road and continue up trail looking out for horses which use this as a bridle path. Dismount when approaching horses and let them know you are there with a friendly greeting. At first T, make a Right. Cross bridge over X-way and make Left, following golf course boundary trail 3/4 mile down hill to it's terminus at Park Boundary Road. Turn Left on to Road - watch for cars!

Make second Right, still on road then travel about 1/4 mile on road, looking for end of grassy section of hillside on Left, where woods begin to extend all the way down to the road. Trailhead is hidden at edge of those woods, about 20 yards up from the road. Trail begins parallel with road but soon turns up the slope. At top of hill, turn right at clearing and follow fun twisting singletrack downhill, across ditch, then Left up bank to road. Cross over guard rail, turn Left on road

19

and take first Left up hill back to far side of Seneca Park Loop loop where you parked your car.

Notes: Seneca is a City of Louisville - Jefferson County Metro Park. The singletrack was built by the Kentucky Mountain Bike Association on a historical trail bed which had been overgrown for generations. A part of this busy urban trail is also a bridle path, so be careful! There are several variations of the loop available, a Left turn at the clearing on top of hill and then keeping to the Right will lead to a short fun singletrack and grassy downhill back to main road. Turn Right on road to return to car.

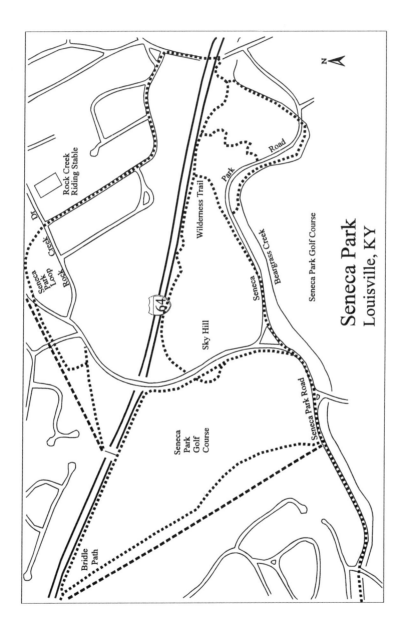

Seneca Park
Louisville, KY

Waverly Park

Rating: Moderate to Advanced.

Trails: 15 miles.

Overview: Fifteen miles of challenging and popular Mountain Bike Trails wind through this quiet, forested, 300 acre Metro Park in south-western Jefferson County. Terrain is hilly and trails are generally quite technical single track built specifically by the Kentucky Mountain Bike Association for mountain bikes. Watch for the occasional outlaw motorcyclist; ATV's came before bicycles here, and have carved quite a few trails of their own in Waverly Park.

Getting There: Take I-65 just South of Louisville to the Outer Loop West. Follow Outer Loop all the way to terminus at 3rd Street Road, make Left, then take Right at stop light: Arnoldtown Road. A few miles on Left is Waverly Park entrance. Park in lot on Right. Trail heads are in several locations throughout the park.

Trail Description: There are a multitude of loops and trails to chose from. The trail that follows the back side of the lake is somewhat less technical than others. The "Dixie Loop" and "Chair Knob Loop" have tough climbs and fast downhills, while the front side trails lead to the awesome climb, "Montana Mountain." The favorite trails, however, are the "Luge" and "Big Ring Ridge" which are fast, wide downhills with banked turns that are vestiges of the ATV's.

For a nice challenging loop, try climbing the trail behind the parking lot and then keep to the right at the top of the hill. Once on this "front side" trail, take a Left at every intersection until you finally cross the road at the very front of the park. Take the trail directly across the road and climb the difficult "Montana Mountain" taking the Right trail half way up the hill. Follow this trail along the side of the ridge until climbing up to the top of "Big Ring Ridge."

Stay on top of the ridge taking the middle trail at the intersections, until you come to a steep five foot dirt ledge on the Right side of the trail, with a less sharp bypass on the Left. A short way past this section is a smaller trail which branches down and to the Right. Take it down then take the first Left, which is "Roman's Ridge" trail. Follow it all the way to the end of the park road.

Notes: The Kentucky Mountain Bike Association have adopted this park and Waverly is popular with the local MTB racing set, so don't be surprised to meet someone with a $2,000 bicycle. Fortunately, the prevalent attitudes don't match the cost of the bikes and friendly riders are the norm, It's a good thing because getting slightly lost is a rite of passage for the Waverly newcomer who does not have a seasoned wheel to follow. The trails are twisty and confusing at first with a lot of short steep climbs to challenge even the very fit. Most of the trails were, after all, built by avid bikers looking for a challenge.

Waverly takes some getting used to, but once you begin to learn the trails and get into shape, it is an incomparable small area mountain bike venue.

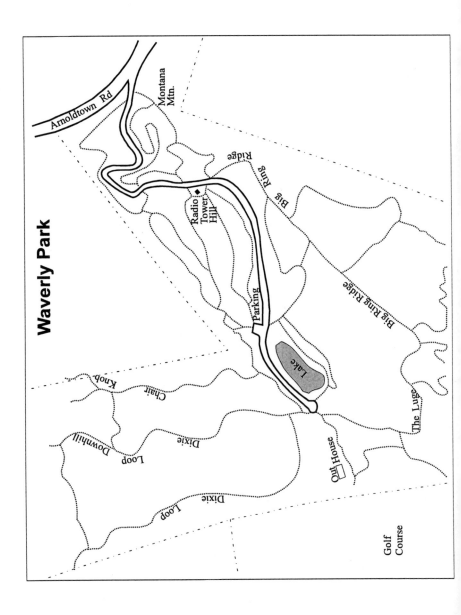

Otter Creek Park

Rating: Easy to Advanced.

Trails: "Blue Trail With Yellow/Red Bypass of Bluff"
9 miles.

Overview: 3000 acre City of Louisville park in Meade County on the Ohio River. The trails consist of superb, wide singletrack through old growth forest, with several challenging technical sections. Beginners should stay on top of the bluff, while advanced riders will enjoy the gnarly downhills leading to Otter Creek. Stay off rest of Yellow and Red trails due to numerous elderly hikers taking part in the Elderhostel programs that run throughout the year.

Getting There: I-265 West all the way to terminus at 31W-60 (Dixie Highway). Head South 13 miles to Muldraugh, in Meade County. Make Right at 1638 at stoplight. Travel 3 miles to Park entrance on Right. Park at Tennis Court / Observatory / Frisbee Golf Course parking lot on Left, or at John Rowe Nature Center on Right. Pick up Blue trailhead where it crosses main road near parking lot. Take Right trailhead if facing park entrance (trail should be traveled counter clockwise if looking at a map).

Trail Description: Follow the Blue trail through cedar and pine forest to first road crossing near park entrance. Watch for traffic! Cross road then bear to left and prepare for steep downhill. A tough climb and another very technical downhill leads to twisting creek-side trail. 1/4 mile past small tower at clearing (stay on blue trail), bear right at the dirt fire road. Cross ravine and take the short steep trail on Left, straight up side of hill. There may be in place a bypass of the ravine to

25

the Left, if so take it. At the Yellow trail, turn Right. Continue climbing, cross bridge and take right at Red trail. At top of bluff, make a left at Blue/Red trail. After several road crossings it will fork Left and become Blue only. Continue until arriving back at John Rowe Nature Center.

Notes: Otter Creek is a fabulous natural retreat. The City of Louisville has shouldered the continuing burden of funding it to the tune of $300,000 per year. The staff are special and their love and devotion for this park is obvious. The lodge and the restaurant are first class places, better than their counterparts in the Kentucky State Parks system.

In the woods, hard and soft wood forest towers over "champagne" single track trails that are over 50 years old. There are plenty of non-bike activities too. Cool off in the clear waters of Otter Creek. Visit the Nature Center. Most of all, show your support of this unique resource by riding responsibly and courteously.

The Kentucky Mountain Bike Association is active in keeping the heavily used Blue trail open to Mountain Bikes. Try this trail during the week to avoid the crowds. The Red/Blue trail at the top of the Bluff/Overlook is the most heavily traveled section by all users. Be courteous to everyone especially the bike-friendly park rangers. The excellent three color map sold at the park store for 25 Cents is a must have for newcomers.

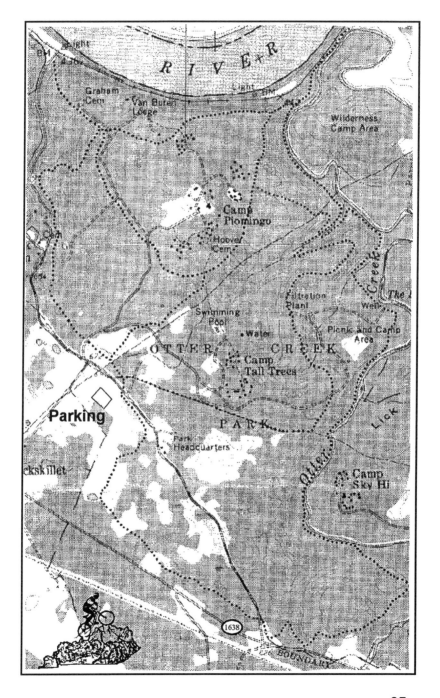

Jefferson County Forest - Horine Section

Rating: Easy - Beginner.

Trails: Fire roads.

Overview: These trails are really dirt and gravel fire roads within the Horine system which provide easy and scenic rides to nowhere. There should be some new trails open to mountain bikes by the Summer of 1995, but check with the ranger first before you ride any. The rest of the Jefferson County Forest trails are, unfortunately, closed to bicycles. Contact the Kentucky Mountain Bike Association for updates.

Getting There: I-265 West to New Cut Road, South. Right at Bear Camp Road, Left at Holsclaw Road. Horine entrance is at top of hill on Right. Stop and check-in at ranger station. They may ask for a couple of dollars if you are there to ride.

Trail Description: The fire road network at Horine extends for several miles past the ranger station. All routes are out and back. Creation of a mountain bike trail network in the Jefferson County Forest is being proposed by the Kentucky Mountain Bike Association to Jefferson County officials. Officials there are also taking seriously the proposal to open some of the existing trails to bikes. These trails are fabulous singletrack and extend for over 15 miles.

Notes: Jefferson County Forest is a system of forested tracts that range across the knobs which form Louisville's southern perimeter. They represent a unique natural and recreational resource that is as yet under utilized. Although bikes are banned from the existing singletrack, bikers are confident that they can achieve approval of an extended trail loop by the Summer of 1995.

Completion of a trail system will depend upon how soon they are allowed to begin work. The Horine area encompasses over 1000 acres and could become a major mountain bike trail system if the County government remains cooperative. The terrain would include an ideal mix of several steep downhills and very long climbs with a nice mix of single track connected by fire roads.

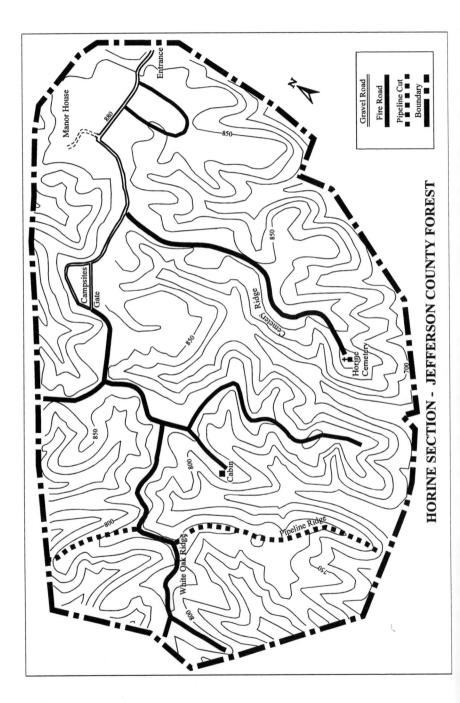

South Park Hills - Brickyards

Rating: Advanced.

Trails: Unknown Distance.

Overview: This semi-private tract adjacent to the Jefferson County Forest is heavily used by motorcyclists during weekend afternoons, although there are plenty of trails to share. Be careful and use your ears! High speed trails with berms and jumps are intermixed with pristine singletrack.

Getting There: I-265 West to National Turnpike South. Make a Left at first stoplight at Fairdale Road. Cross railroad tracks and make first Right on South Park Road. Take second Left past Golf Course onto Granger Road. Park at end of Granger Road away from private homes. Trail head is at end of road.

Trail Description: High speed ATV trails rise up and along the ridge lines. Once past the difficult climb to the top, numerous spur trails feed into the main ridge trail.

Notes: The brick yard adjoins a huge clay pit with lots of ramps and jumps. Be careful!

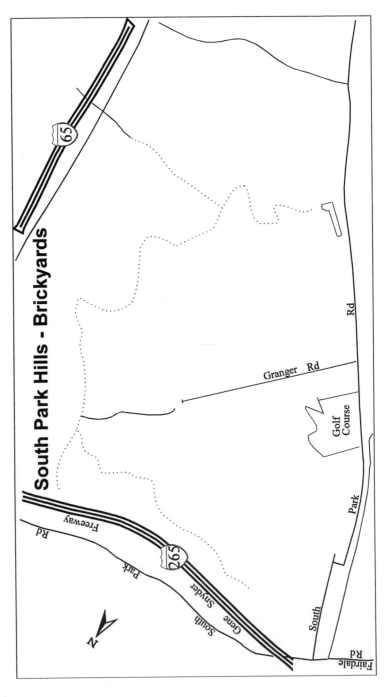

South Park Hills - Brickyards

Golf Course

Granger Rd

Gene Snyder Freeway

Fairdale Rd

Fort Duffield Park

Rating: Moderate to Advanced.

Trails: 5 miles.

Overview: This 200 acre park in the city of West Point, just West of Louisville, offers a 4 mile loop up and over a 250 vertical foot hill. Some of the trail is still under construction at this writing but is scheduled to be complete by the summer of 1995.

The Blue (bicycle) Trail was still under construction at the time of publication. It is a one way 4 mile loop. Numerous trail signs and markers show the way. The trail climbs the main hill which at 200 feet plus, dominates the region and overlooks West Point. It is a real tough climb. The rest of the trail is mainly smooth technical singletrack, with some fun downhill sections.

Getting There: Take I-265 West to its terminus at the junction with 31-W. Take 31-W, West, towards Fort Knox and Otter Creek Park, until you reach the town of West Point. After the traffic light, look for the small sign on the Left and turn there. Follow the road to the Right, through the gate and park in the parking lot. The trailheads are marked with signs, there is a short hiking only trail (orange). The bike trail is marked in blue.

Trail Description: Climb the access road on the Left to the top of the hill. If a singletrack bypass trail has been constructed by the time you are there, take it instead. The access road is generally closed to all private vehicles including bicycles but park officials will make an exception until the access trail is complete. At the top of the hill you will see Fort Duffield. Keep on the Blue Trail, following the ridge. Be sure to stop for the great view. The Blue trail will begin a torturous descent to the Right, which after several miles will bring you back to the road, close to the parking lot.

Notes: Fort Duffield, a Union outpost during the Civil War, is at the top of the hill and is the largest Civil War earthen fort in Kentucky. Trenches in the battlements above are as deep as 25 feet and are remarkably well preserved due to the fact that the site lay undisturbed for over 150 years. Fort Duffield is a City of West Point park and is fully funded by the city, which is trying to revitalize it's historic downtown by promoting tourism. The bike trail was funded by a federal grant for that purpose. Almost 200 years old, the city was one of the first shipping outposts on the down river side of the Falls of the Ohio, and Louisville.

As a result of the hard work of local activists and historians, Fort Duffield is poised to become a major civil war attraction and mountain bike venue. City officials and the park custodians hope that mountain bikers will return to appreciate the manifest historical and cultural offerings of this venerable town and unique park.

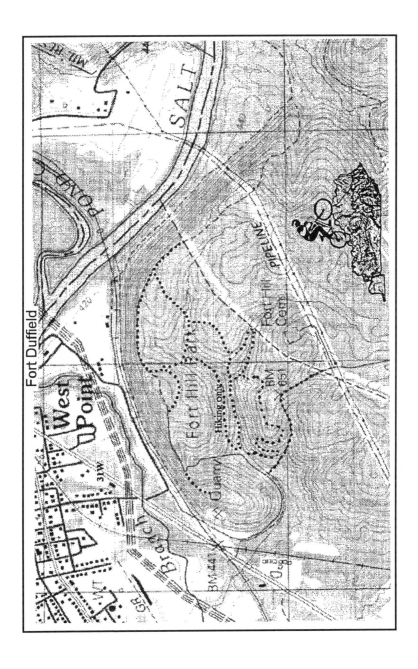

Central Kentucky Trails

Although there is not an abundance of public land in Central Kentucky, there is plenty of good riding for the informed mountain biker. State Parks and management areas operated by the Department of Fish and Wildlife comprise the majority of the public lands in the region. The moderate terrain of most of Central Kentucky gives way to bluffs and nobs of up to 200 vertical feet of climbing in many of these rugged areas; good for the deer and the mountain bikers!

Mountain Biking in Kentucky

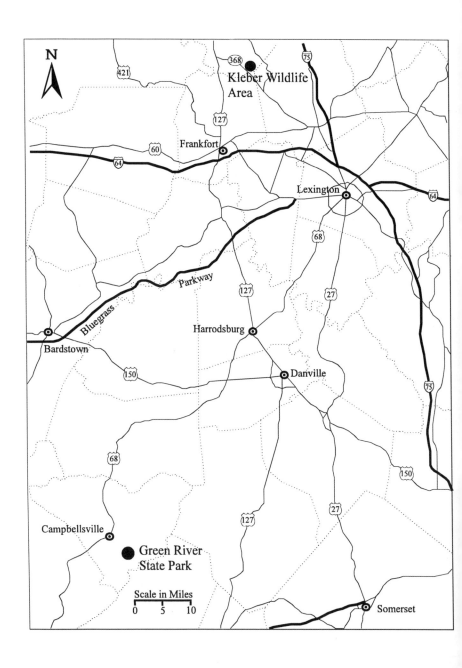

Kleber Fish and Wildlife Preserve

Rating: Advanced.

Trails: "Front Loop" 11 miles.

Overview: Very challenging and hilly singletrack with a return leg on a rough gravel and dirt road. Rocky, challenging downhills punctuate grueling climbs which are notable for their duration. Although everything at Kleber is ridable, the level of exertion required should give the unfit rider pause. The area is remote and suitable precautions must be taken such as carrying tools and first aid. There are no facilities, water must be brought in.

Getting There: I-64 to Frankfort, exit 127 North and go straight through town, towards Owenton. On 127 go through Swallowfield, then look for 368 in about five miles. Right on 368 then about seven miles to Kleber Ranger Station on Right. 1/10 mile past station is unmarked gravel road on Left. Turn there and park at grassy clearing on Left.

Trail Description: Trailhead is on Left about 1/4 mile down gravel road from 368. It begins in a stand of cedar trees and climbs straight up hillside to grassy "road" at top of ridge. Make a Right and travel a short distance until trail turns to the Right down the hill and into the woods. Steep downhill across ditch and back up, keeping to Right at top. Back down difficult rocky trail back to gravel road. Left on road, up short, steep hill, then Left onto singletrack, climbing up through woods. Look for 90 degree Left turn after trail flattens out, then two downhills to creek crossing and same gravel road. Left on road then another Left at next trailhead up through woodsy, fun singletrack and back to road. Left on gravel road down steep gravel hill, then Left at trailhead just past the bottom of the hill, into the woods. Up and down a few times through the tight singletrack then a sharp left after clearing the woods down very steep hill to road. Another Left on road to first grassy-dirt track Left that cuts back up hill. Long open climb toward distant field row, then Right - Left into woods and down ravine. At top of other side there are two more ravines on a grassy trail, then bear Right for long grassy downhill to Road. Take Right and return to car on gravel road.

Notes: Kleber is a Kentucky Fish and Wildlife property of over 2400 acres. These areas can be found throughout Kentucky and are funded by the sale of hunting and fishing licenses. This infamously difficult trail was opened by local racers Larry Reynolds and Bob Moss, who train on it weekly. Be forewarned that you will probably get lost the first time unless you ride with an experienced guide. If you do, you have only to turn to your Right down the bluff to find the gravel access road which runs the length of the area. The Kentucky Mountain Bike Association do conduct monthly rides there which would be a good opportunity to learn the trail. The difficulty of this trail is made up for by the good views, sense of accomplishment and fun downhills. There is a another loop adding 7 miles to the trail but this is partially on private land and best left to the locals. Stay away from this popular deer hunting destination during gun season. There are a lot of ticks here during the early Summer, so bring plenty of repellent.

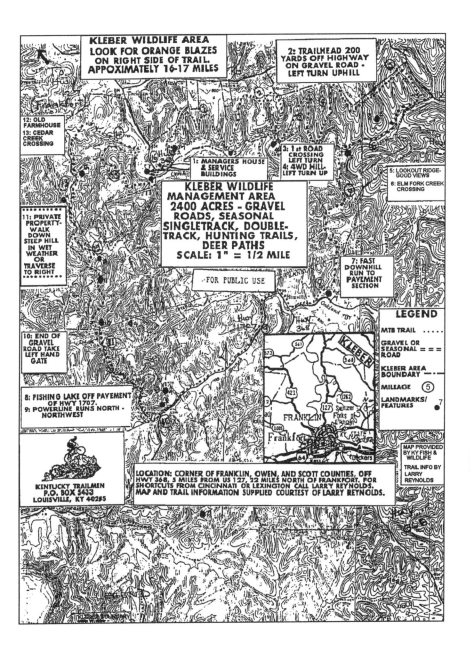

KLEBER WILDLIFE AREA LOOK FOR ORANGE BLAZES ON RIGHT SIDE OF TRAIL. APPOXIMATELY 16-17 MILES

2: TRAILHEAD 200 YARDS OFF HIGHWAY ON GRAVEL ROAD - LEFT TURN UPHILL

12: OLD FARMHOUSE
13: CEDAR CREEK CROSSING

1: MANAGERS HOUSE & SERVICE BUILDINGS

3: 1st ROAD CROSSING LEFT TURN
4: 4WD HILL LEFT TURN UP

5: LOOKOUT RIDGE- GOOD VIEWS
6: ELM FORK CREEK CROSSING

KLEBER WILDLIFE MANAGEMENT AREA 2400 ACRES - GRAVEL ROADS, SEASONAL SINGLETRACK, DOUBLE-TRACK, HUNTING TRAILS, DEER PATHS
SCALE: 1" = 1/2 MILE

11: PRIVATE PROPERTY- WALK DOWN STEEP HILL IN WET WEATHER OR TRAVERSE TO RIGHT

-FOR PUBLIC USE

7: FAST DOWNHILL RUN TO PAVEMENT SECTION

LEGEND

MTB TRAIL . . . . .

10: END OF GRAVEL ROAD TAKE LEFT HAND GATE

GRAVEL OR SEASONAL = = = ROAD

KLEBER AREA BOUNDARY — · —

MILEAGE ⑤

8: FISHING LAKE OFF PAVEMENT OF HWY 1707.
9: POWERLINE RUNS NORTH - NORTHWEST

LANDMARKS/ FEATURES ● 7

KENTUCKY TRAILMEN P.O. BOX 5433 LOUISVILLE, KY 40255

MAP PROVIDED BY KY FISH & WILDLIFE

TRAIL INFO BY LARRY REYNOLDS

LOCATION: CORNER OF FRANKLIN, OWEN, AND SCOTT COUNTIES, OFF HWY 368, 5 MILES FROM US 127, 22 MILES NORTH OF FRANKFORT. FOR SHORTCUTS FROM CINCINNATI OR LEXINGTON CALL LARRY REYNOLDS. MAP AND TRAIL INFORMATION SUPPLIED COURTESY OF LARRY REYNOLDS.

41

Fort Hill State Park

Rating: Moderate to Advanced.

Trails: 8 miles.

Overview: A riotous mix of twisting singletrack and formidable hill climbs and down hills. This park in the heart of Frankfort is a favorite with the local BMX crowd, also known as the "Moving Targets" by virtue of the fact that a public archery range also exists in the park. Be careful of the practicing archers and of any illegal hunters, specially around hunting season.

Getting there: Taking Highway 127 into Frankfort, cross the distinctive double bridges and then take a Left into the Capitol Plaza parking lot. Fort Hill rises above you from the back of the parking lot.

Trail Description: There is no way to describe the serpentine trails which wind around and up and down this massif which dominates the Frankfort skyline. Simply get on the trail and start riding.

Notes: Do not disturb the remnants of the old Civil War fortifications at the top which gave this mountain it's name. Use caution on the steep downhill sections and be aware that there are a lot of thorn bushes here. Patch kits are essential equipment, and flat proofing for your tires and tubes, in it's variety of forms, is strongly recommended and practiced by locals.

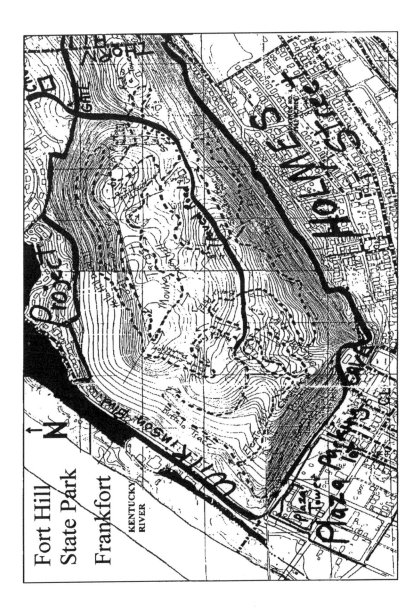

Fort Hill State Park
Frankfort

KENTUCKY RIVER

N

Green River State Park

Rating: Moderate.

Trails: Green River Dam Trail (uncompleted) 7 miles.

Overview: A small but active group of mountain bikers in the Danville, and Campbellsville area have worked with park officials at Green River State Park to create a trail system near Green River Lake. The short term goal of the group is to complete a trail all the way to the dam, which would create a loop over 10 miles long. Local riders also use the Green River ATV park which is a few miles to the South. The trails in the dam area are experimental and subject to review by the State Parks officials.

Getting There: From I-64, at the Frankfort/Lawrenceburg Exit 59, take Highway 127, South, to Harrodsburg. Take 68, South/West to Campbellsville, then Route 55, South to the Green River Lake State Park.

Trail Description: This is another developmental trail which is not complete at the time of this writing but should be by the time it is ready for distribution. The trail is a result of the efforts of the small but active Central Kentucky Chapter of the Kentucky Mountain Bike Association. The trail is technical singletrack. The trailhead should be marked at the Park. Check with a ranger if you cannot find the trail.

Notes: This area is the historical heartland of Kentucky. Of considerable interest is the Perryville Battlefield, at Perryville, Kentucky, on the junction of Highway 58 and 150. Here was fought the largest Civil War battle in Kentucky. Abraham Lincoln's childhood home, Old Fort

Harrod from the eighteenth century, and My Old Kentucky Home, the place made famous as the home of Steven Foster, are all within a 45 minute drive of the Green River Lake State Park.

Eddy O's Bike Shop, 502-789-4330, should be able to provide more information about local trail conditions.

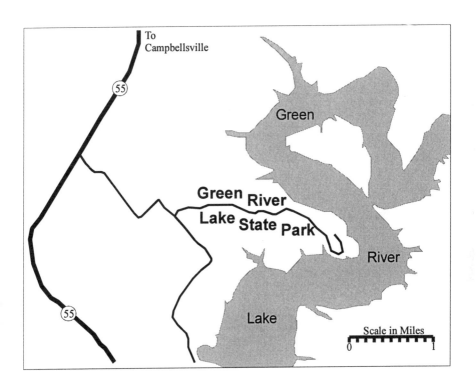

Green River State Park - ATV Park

Rating: Moderate.

Trails: Unknown distance.

Overview: The ATV park is busy with motorized users during the weekend; however, once you have ventured past the trailhead, the motorists spread out quite a bit and there is little potential for conflict between the motorized users and bicyclists.

Getting There: Just a few miles South of Campbellsville, on Highway 76.

Trail Description: ATV trails are always wider than hiking or bicycle singletrack for obvious reasons. The trail system here is very extensive and varied. However, as with most ATV areas there are plenty of opportunities to "get air" and go fast, but the trails further back are surprisingly pristine. It's important to keep track of where you are going.

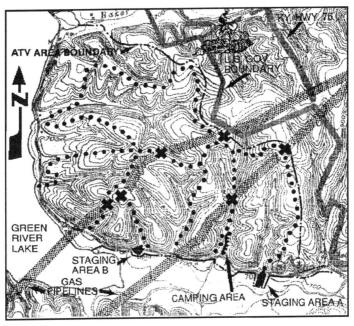

GREEN RIVER LAKE, KY ATV AREA

LEGEND

 PIPELINE CLEARING
• • • • MARKED ATV TRAILS
✗ PIPELINE CROSSING
ATV AREA BOUNDARY
SCALE = 1000 FEET

Northern Kentucky Trails

This region includes the Cincinnati Metro Area, which, taken from the standpoint of mountain bike enthusiasts, gives it the highest population density in Kentucky. There is a scarcity of places to ride here, however, due to the lack of public land on the Kentucky side, and the shortsighted highhandedness of public officials in Cincinnati, who long ago banned bicycles from every city and county park!

Active off road cyclists in Northern Kentucky had been forced to travel several hours by car to reach legal riding areas, or, to make due with a few tracts of private land where riding on the one or two miles of trail available was tolerated. This obviously unsatisfactory situation stifled the development of the sport in an area which was physically replete with ideal forested terrain. Bikers in Cincinnati on the Ohio side, and Convington, Erlanger, Burlington, Fort Thomas and all the other thriving communities in Kentucky, were frustrated by serious land access problems.

Into this situation have stepped the Northern Kentucky Chapter of the Kentucky Mountain Bike Association, which organized in the Fall of 1994 to address the dearth of places to ride in their area. So far, through their hard work, Northern Kentucky has already obtained an excellent venue: Middle Creek Park, near Burlington, Kentucky.

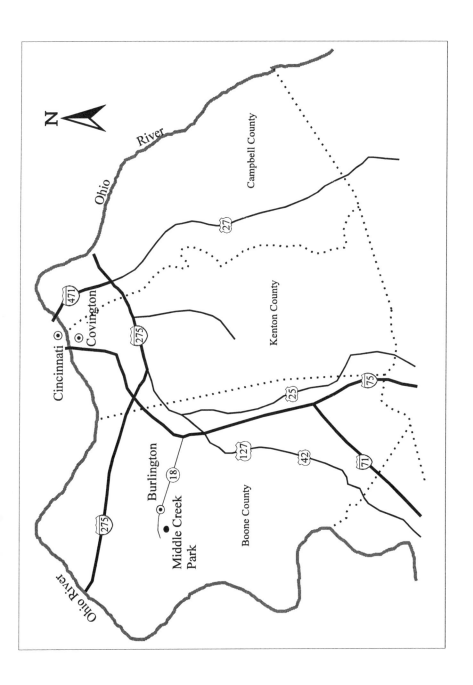

Middle Creek Park

Rating: Moderate.

Trails: 5 miles.

Overview: Rolling singletrack in a county park less than 30 minutes from I-71.

Getting There: I-71 to exit on Burlington Pike (Route 18). Head West toward historic Burlington which is a County Seat. Pass through town and continue on until you see the signs for the Dinsmore Homestead on the Right. Middle Creek Park entrance is just on the other side of the road, on the Left. Park in the unpaved lot.

Trail Description: There is a large wooden trail map at the parking lot. All trails here are open to bikes. The trail system consists of a perimeter loop of 3 miles with 5 crossing trails. Start with the rough climb up the ridge and follow the nice trail along the ridge until it drops down into another valley. Another difficult climb leads to the second ridge trail. A rough descent to the creek bed completes the main loop.

Notes: Two local Boy Scouts recently rehabbed the trails as part of their requirements for reaching Eagle Scout. Subsequently, the Northern Kentucky Mountain Bike Association have helped maintain the extensive park trail system. Horses use the trails so be careful and show courtesy when approaching them. Remember that many times horses view mountain bikes as predators! At the end of the final downhill is private property, which you can easily stray into if you miss the turn. Try not to trespass, especially since the land is used as a private hunting club!

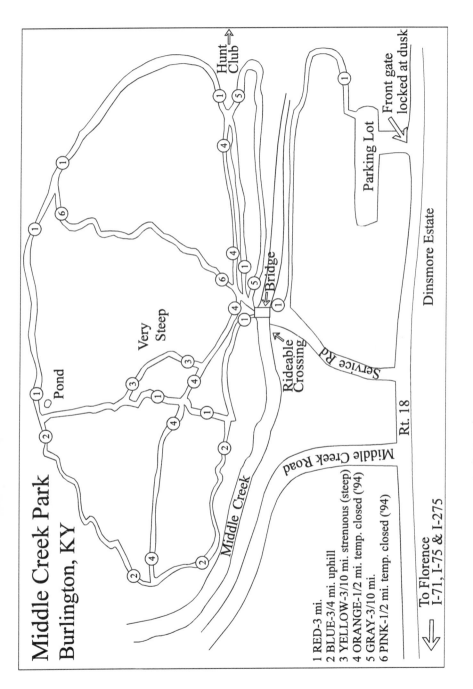

Middle Creek Park
Burlington, KY

Pond

Very
Steep

Hunt
Club

Front gate
locked at dusk

Parking Lot

Dinsmore Estate

Bridge

Rideable
Crossing

Service Rd.

Rt. 18

Middle Creek Road

Middle Creek

To Florence
I-71, I-75 & I-275

1 RED-3 mi.
2 BLUE-3/4 mi. uphill
3 YELLOW-3/10 mi. strenuous (steep)
4 ORANGE-1/2 mi. temp. closed ('94)
5 GRAY-3/10 mi.
6 PINK-1/2 mi. temp. closed ('94)

Cave Run Lake

Operated by the United States Corps of Engineers, the lake was created by damming the upper portion of the Licking River in 1974. Surrounded by hardwood forested hills, and bisected by the Sheltowee Trace, the Cave Run area is replete with excellent trails. Cave Run has been featured in several MTB publications as a little known but desirable riding location. The more popular trails, such as Caney Loop, are in fact fairly busy; however, some excellent and remote singletrack exists close by.

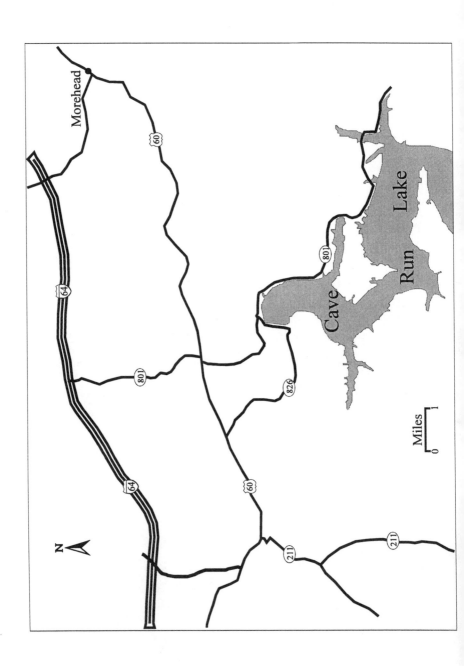

Caney Loop Trail

Rating: Moderate.

Trails: 12 miles.

Overview: Fast, rolling, wide, singletrack with moderate climbs.

Getting There: Follow I-64 East of Lexington and Mount Sterling. Take 801 South at exit # 133. Follow 801 across U.S. 60 all the way to Cave Run Dam. Make Right at 826, crossing dam, and park at Stony Cove. Trailhead is gravel road at end of second parking lot.

Trail Description: Climb short gravel hill a few hundred yards looking for Caney Loop trail head on Left. Caney Loop gradually climbs along lakeside for a little over 6 miles. Take Right at Sheltowee Trace, which is marked with distinctive white turtle symbols and diamonds on trees. If you take the power line cut which is just before the Sheltowee trace intersection, you will have to descend and climb some very steep hills before reaching the Sheltowee. Sheltowee Trace returns to the parking lot on a slightly more inland path leading to the original gravel road. Make a Left at the road to return to parking lot. Motorized vehicles are allowed on Sheltowee so watch out! The loop may be cut in half by initially following the trailhead gravel road until it becomes singletrack and ends at the Sheltowee Trace. Make a Right and follow the Trace around back to the gravel road as in the description above.

Notes: This is the most popular trail in Cave Run and it shows. Use good judgment by not riding when the trail is wet. Horses abound during the weekend, so respect their natural skittishness by dismounting when approaching. The Caney Loop is an excellent and less challenging alternative to the other hillier and more technical trails at the Zilpo Camp and Pioneer Weapons Area.

See map for Zilpo / Pioneer Weapons Hunting Area

Zilpo / Pioneer Weapons Hunting Area

Rating: Advanced.

Trails: 16 miles.

Overview: South of the Caney Loop and accessed from the Zilpo Campground is a trail network favored by Cave Run regulars. The Buckskin (9 miles), Cave Run (4 miles) and Hog Pen (3 miles) trails can be connected to make several challenging loops winding through the 7,000 acre Pioneer Weapons Hunting Area, which is managed by the Department of Fish and wildlife.

Getting There: From I-64 East, take exit # 123 turning Right onto U.S. 60. Follow U.S. 60 for 5 miles, turning Right at Salt Lick onto route 211. Turn Left at Forest Service Road 129/918 after about 3 miles. Follow 918 to end at Zilpo Campground. Trailhead for Buckskin Trail is well marked at campground.

Trail Description: Picking up the Buckskin Trail (trail # 113) at the Zilpo Trailhead, travel West near lakeshore. The loop trails: Connector (#108), Hog Pen (#106) and Cave Run (#112) are on the Left and cut South toward the Zilpo Scenic Byway, FS 918, leading back toward the campground.

Notes: These trails are more challenging than the Caney Loop. They are also more scenic and less crowded. The singletrack is narrow and rocky with a lot of hills. The climbs are not too severe on the lower Buckskin Trail but get more challenging as one rides further away from the Zilpo peninsula. For a trail epic, try a point to point ride from Zilpo, along the Buckskin, then connecting up with the

Sheltowee just South of the Caney Loop and, finally, along Caney loop trail to the Stony Cove parking area (See description for Caney Loop Trail).

Many of these trails and others can also be accessed from the Clear Creek campground. A number of different combinations are also possible using the Scenic Byway, Forest Service Road 918, as a return leg to the Zilpo Campground.

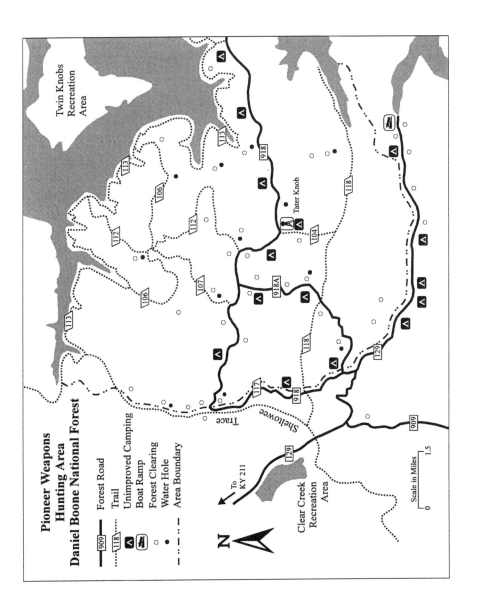

Sheltowee, North of the Dam

Rating: Advanced.

Trails: 10 miles.

Getting There: Follow route 801 south from I-64 to the dam, park at High Bank Picnic Area on Right. Sheltowee Trailhead crosses 801, just East of the dam.

Trail Description: Follow Sheltowee North, away from the lake. Big Limestone (trail # 109) meets the Sheltowee on the Right and ends on Forest Service Road #16. The trail ends at U.S. 60 after a little over 10 miles of singletrack and big hills. A left on U.S. 60 and another Left on 801 will bring you back to High Bank Picnic Area.

Notes: This is another "local knowledge" trail for fit riders. This part of the Sheltowee is also open to ATV's and horses so be careful. It is possible to pick up the Sheltowee again off U.S. 60 and follow it North, across I-64 and to the town of Morehead. The distance involved would necessitate at least one night of camping, however. Be advised that U.S. 60 is a fairly busy road with truck traffic.

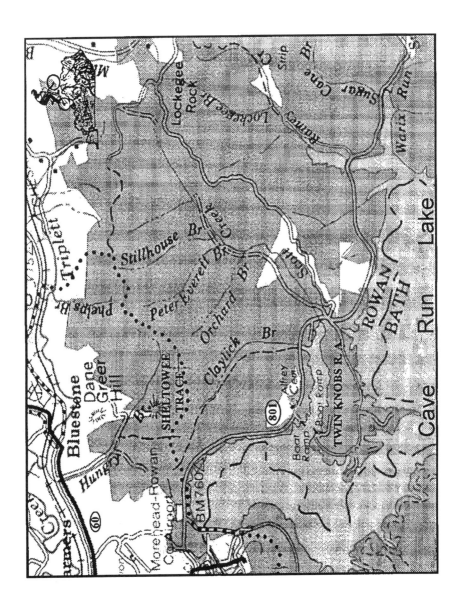

Red River Gorge

The Red River Gorge has become famous for the great rock climbing there, but it offers the same kind of opportunity to the savvy mountain biker. The trails in this region are just beginning to be explored and developed for MTB. Consider what Moab, Utah was like ten years ago for mountain biking and you will have an idea of the possibilities which exist at the Red River Gorge.

On the down side, the Clifty Wilderness Area, the developed trails in the Red River Gorge Geological Area, and the trails in the Natural Bridge State Park, are all off-limits to bicycles. Tickets for riding in off limits areas can range from $25 to $100 dollars and repeat offenders can be arrested.

The Federal Rangers are sympathetic to mountain bikers but they have a job to do, especially in the Wilderness Area, where not even the rangers are allowed to use mechanical devices of any sort. It is up to the individual to be aware of boundaries. This still leaves thousands of acres and hundreds of miles of trails in this beautiful region wide open to bicycles.

The topography in this area is unique and should be discussed as it relates to the safety of the trail system. Long ridges, each one lined with broken walls of lime and sand stone, a few dozen to a few hundred feet high, criss cross the entire valley of the Red River, creating what we call the Gorge. The multitude of these rock walls is what makes the area so attractive to climbers.

Any trail which runs perpendicular to the ravine must travel through breaks in the ridge top cliffs in order to reach the top. As a practical matter this means that any "bush whacking" will require a certain amount of mountaineering skills to overcome the hidden ridge walls. If you stray off the trail be prepared to be frustrated from reaching your target by an insurmountable cliff.

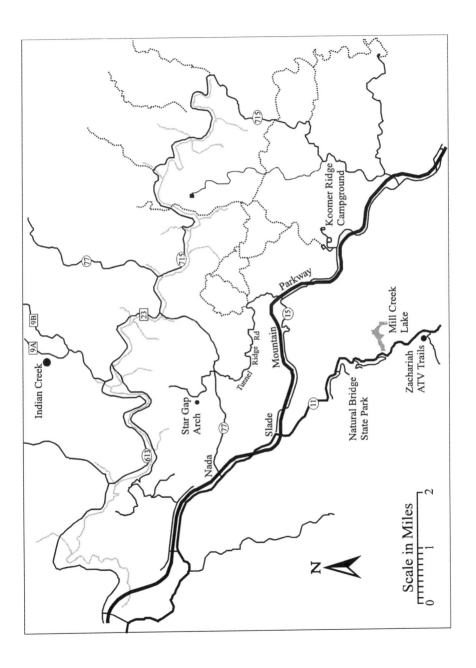

Zachariah ATV trails

Rating: Moderate to Advanced.

Trails: 12 miles.

Overview: Untold miles of ATV trails and Forest Service roads lie between the town of Zachariah and Natural Bridge State Park. Remember: Natural Bridge Park itself is off limits to bicycles. Watch for motorized vehicles and realize that you are in an isolated area and must take the required precautions of extra tools, first aid kit etc..

Getting There: Follow the Bert Combs Mountain Parkway off of I-64 East of Lexington. Take the Slade Exit and turn Right toward Natural Bridge State Park. Park on the Right side of road, at the first gravel road past the State Park. This is the trailhead.

Trail Description: Cross the creek just past the trailhead and follow the ATV trail up the mountain. After climbing for over a mile, the trail will top out on a ridge and continue to the Right along the ridge top. The fourth trail on the Right should be the Sheltowee Trace. Make sure by identifying the tell-tale white paint marks on the trees which are either turtles or diamonds. Take the Trace.

After crossing a scenic vista area called the White Branch Arch Narrows, continue on for less than a mile and look to the Right for a somewhat hidden trailhead. Take the trail to a sign marking the State Park boundary and keep Right being careful not to cross Left into the State Park. Follow the trail down until getting to the State Park and immediately dismount and walk the last few hundred yards to the Road.

At the Road, turn Right and ride about a mile until you get back to the parked cars.

Notes: The initial climb up to the ridge is over a mile long and of "world class" caliber. Be sure to stop at the look-out and take in the view which stretches for miles on both sides of the trail.

It is important to realize that this area represents scores of miles of trail, and the loop described above is only the tip of the proverbial iceberg. Get a good topographic map and explore the trails yourself. You will probably meet some ATV's but this area is so large there is little danger of conflict or collision. Don't forget to stop for pizza at Miguel's, a local climbers hangout and pizzeria, on the way back to the Parkway.

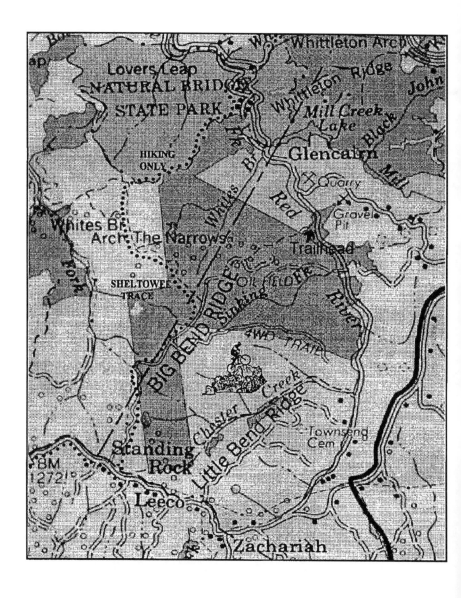

Indian Creek

Rating: Moderate.

Trails: 30 miles.

Overview: These trails, in the North West sector of the Gorge, are scenic, not too difficult, and very wet! Every possible loop entails riding through some creek/trails with water from a few inches to a few feet deep. None of the creeks are particularly fast moving, however, and the danger level is low. The most important tactics for creek riding are keeping your weight back, maintaining momentum through the water, and looking ahead to avoid large rocks.

Getting There: At the Slade Exit to the Mountain Parkway, go Left towards Red River Gorge Geological Area. Follow the signs to the Gorge going through the shanty town of Nada (pronounced Nay-da). Pass through the one-lane Nada tunnel, not forgetting to turn your lights on when in the old logging tunnel. Make a Left at the Iron Bridge and continue on for a few miles to Forest Service Road 9 on the Left. A short distance up the road is the intersection of 9A and 9B; take 9A, Left. Park 1/4 mile further up 9A, at a widening in the road near large boulders set alongside the road.

Trail Description: The Powder Mill bicycle trail begins on the Left (creek) side of the Road, doubling back on along Indian Creek for 100 yards until it crosses and goes up the hill. Follow Powder Mill trail up the hill as it winds for a few miles to the top of Hatton's Ridge. Go Right onto the fast and wide Hatton's Ridge Trail. Follow Hatton's Ridge as it gradually widens and becomes a gravel/dirt road. Make the first Right that is a real road. This is a severe 90° turn down

71

the ridge. Follow the downhill to the blacktop road and make a Right. About 1/3 mile down blacktop, Leatherwood Branch/Forest Service Road 9A, is the first gravel road on Right. The road soon narrows to an ATV path as it runs in and out of Leatherwood Branch. This is the same road which you parked on.

Notes: An examination of the map will show that this is only one of several possible routes. You can, for instance, descend Hatton's ridge traveling south by taking the Right fork. Powder Mill is sometimes used by horses and may be chopped up quite a bit if the ground is soft. 9B also runs in and out of the creek as does the Indian Creek Trail proper which begins at the 9A bridge about a mile North of the intersection with 9B. Because of the wetness you will be well advised to avoid these trails during cold weather. But you should also be aware that Indian Creek is a popular party place in the Gorge and there will be plenty of people and vehicles parked on the side of the road during peak season in the Summer.

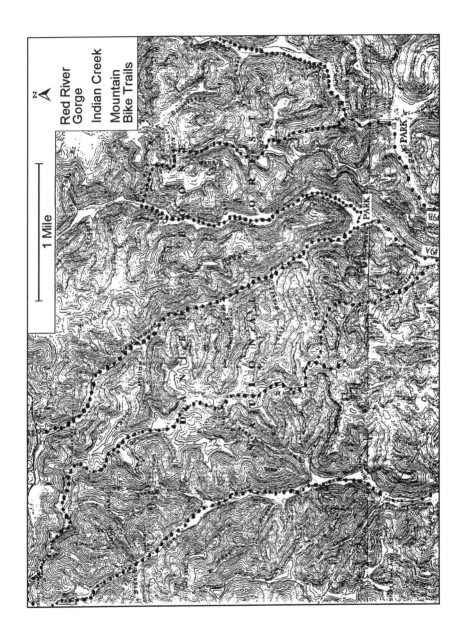

Red River
Gorge

Indian Creek

Mountain
Bike Trails

N

1 Mile

Star Gap Arch Trail

Rating: Advanced.

Trails: 8 miles out and back.

Overview: Warning! watch for cliffs at end of spur trails.

A truly unique trail which provides great views of Star Gap Arch from both sides! Rocky and steep, the trail traverses a sharp ridge which in places narrows to a few feet on each side. With rocky ledges and scenic views, it reminds some people of mountain bike trails in Utah.

This trail is just on the other side of the Geological Area boundary and is in the heart of the scenic Red River Gorge formations but is O.K. to ride. It is difficult and unimproved but very scenic and could well become the premier trail in the Gorge area if shown a little TLC, and extended down to the valley to become a loop.

Getting There: From the Slade Exit of the Mountain Parkway, follow the signs to the Gorge, taking a Right at the first intersection, then traveling East on State Road 15, until you see the gravel Tunnel Ridge Road on the Left. You will also see the trailhead for the Sheltowee Trace on the Right. Take Tunnel Ridge Road until you see the sign for Star Gap. There are two trailheads on the Left side, about 1/5 mile apart, take the first one.

Trail Description: Keep bearing to the Right, you will come to a private campground which is all right to cross. Be careful, since the spur trails often lead to cliff drop offs. After about two miles you will come to a steep saddle in the ridge and have to carry your bike down a six foot ledge. The trail ends on top of the a rock spire at the terminus of the ridge. There is a game trail which continues down the toe of the bluff, slightly to the Left, but it is unexplored. The Red River is down below there, somewhere...

Notes: The forest ranger has tried to discourage riders from attempting to travel off the ridge and try to link with the trails and roads in the Red River valley. He is afraid that riders will trespass or get hurt. The Kentucky Mountain Bike Association intends to try anyway. There are probably some large cliffs to be negotiated around, and there are some very territorial land owners in this area; nevertheless, if a trail link from the end of the Star Gap trail to the trails at the bottom of the valley could be achieved, the resulting loop would be unlike anything else found in Kentucky. Doing so would require some careful preparation with map and compass to make sure that you did not stray onto private land.

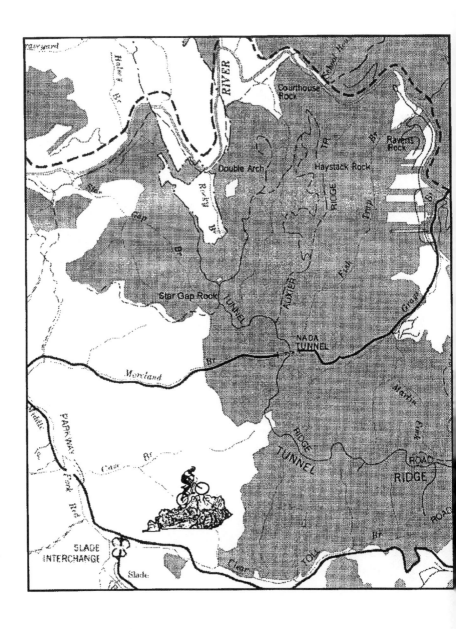

Sheltowee Trace National Recreation Trail

While many of the rides that are discussed in other chapters of this book include portions of the Sheltowee Trace, this chapter comprises rides which are totally or mostly on the Sheltowee Trace. These trails are along especially nice sections of this 250 mile trail which runs North and South along the entire length of the Daniel Boone National Forest.

Sheltowee was the explorer and frontiersman Daniel Boone's Native American name, given to him when he was adopted into the Shawnee tribe by Chief Blackfish. It means Big Turtle. The Sheltowee Trace memorializes a North-South route that was in existence before Daniel Boone explored Kentucky, and is now marked along it's entire length by distinctive white turtle symbols, or by simple white diamonds. It is open to bikes except where it passes through the Red River Gorge Geological Area and the Clifty Wilderness.

The trail can only be characterized by its variety, which includes every type of trail surface from blacktop roadway to narrow singletrack, and moderate to mountainous terrain. In some places, the Trace is merely a designation of blacktop or gravel road, in others it is pristine singletrack.

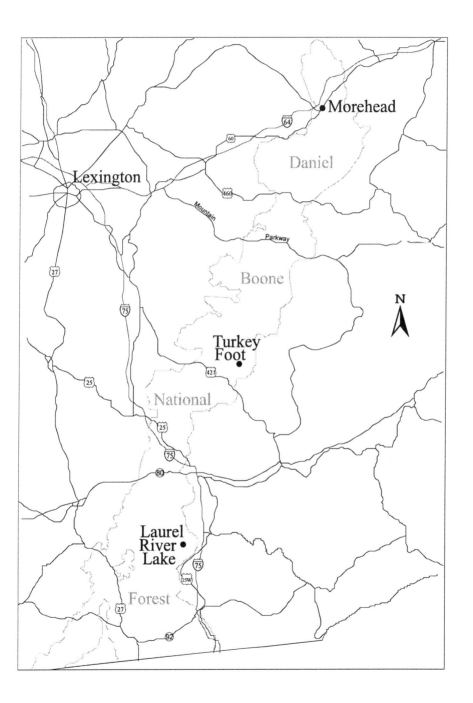

Turkey Foot to Arvel Section

Rating: Moderate to Advanced.

Trails: 10 miles.

Overview: This very nice section of the Sheltowee Trace, in the heart of Eastern Kentucky, has long, moderate climbs but is technically challenging, narrow singletrack with rocks and other obstacles continually demanding the rider's attention.

Getting There: I-71 South of Lexington to the town of Berea. At the Berea Exit, take route 21 through town to State Road 421 South. At the Town of McKee, take a Left onto Route 89. Travel 3 miles until you see the Recreation Area sign at the forest service road on the Right.

Trail Description: Follow the singletrack trail all the way to the road at Arvel. The return leg by pavement is 7.5 miles.

Notes: ATV's are not allowed on this section of the Trace, making it a somewhat unique narrow singletrack section. Unfortunately, a mud slide last year took out several hundred yards of trail. Crossing it means negotiating a maddening maze of fallen timber and brush. There is a meadow section which has very tall grass during the summer, with some briars. These obstacles should not deter the determined mountain biker, since the rest of the trail is champagne singletrack, albeit a little on the "wild side."

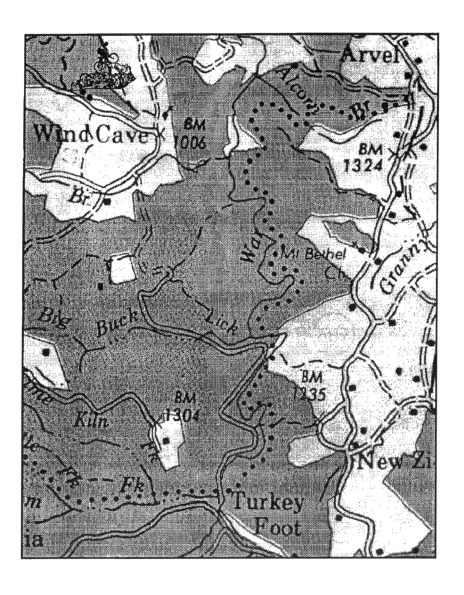

Northern Terminus to Morehead

Rating: Advanced.

Trails: 20 miles, one way.

Overview: Much of this section of the Sheltowee Trace is little used singletrack, providing both the benefits of isolation and the burden of forced portages around fallen timber and impenetrable overgrowth.

Getting There: East on I-64 past Mount Sterling, take exit 137 at Morehead. Travel North on Route 2 for a short distance until reaching Route 377, turn Right. Go 20 miles on 377, following the same valley that the Sheltowee Trace does, until you reach the parking lot and the trailhead for the Northern Terminus of the 250 mile long trail.

Trail Description: ATV's use the trail here and the path is fairly wide and rocky as it climbs up to the ridge top for half a mile. Rolling wide singletrack follows the ridge line for several miles on a trail made fairly rough by the motorized vehicles. At 10 miles the trail narrows considerably and climbs up and down the ridge until crossing Route 779 at Holly Fork. Soon you will come to a narrow suspension bridge on cables that sways considerably as you cross it!

Past the swinging bridge, the trail degrades into undergrowth and all but the hardiest bikers will turn around and take 799 West to 377 back to the original trailhead. One can also bypass the overgrown section by taking 799 South until it picks up the Trace again, just past the I-64 crossing. Here the Sheltowee follows gravel road 977. Two spurs connect the

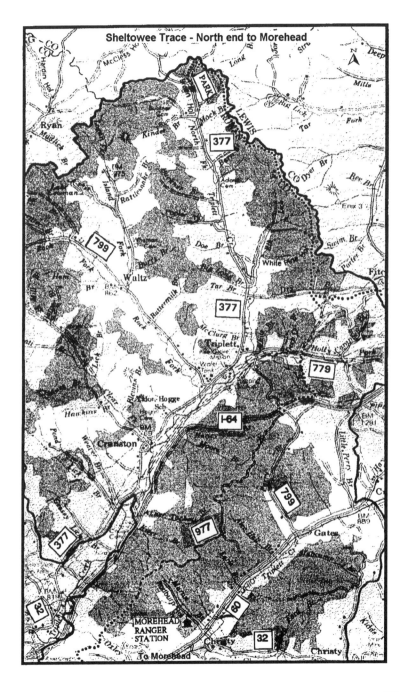

trail from 977 to Rodburn Hollow and Morehead State University.

Notes: Side trails include the previously mentioned Rodburn Hollow and the Jenny Wiley National Recreation Trail which runs into the Sheltowee just after the trail crossing at White Pine Hollow.

Laurel River Lake/Holly Bay Recreation Area

Rating: Beginner / Moderate.

Trails: Unknown Distance.

Overview: Easy portions of the Sheltowee Trace and spur trails make this a readily accessible fun trail. Take note that this area is very close to the Big South Fork Recreation Area.

Getting There: Take I-75 South, to Corbin, Kentucky. Exit at Highway 312, West, into the Daniel Boone National Forest. Take the road Left to the Holly Bay Recreation Area and park.

Trail Description: Pick up the Sheltowee Trace where it crosses the road. We can not recommend any trails here, since we don't know the area well.

Notes: A U.S. Geological Survey Topographical Map which included Laurel River Lake would be an asset here since there are no mountain bike maps and no local clubs or bike shops to call. This area was included in the book because of all the favorable reports that have been made over the last few years of the riding potential, and the moderate but very wild terrain.

Cumberland Falls State Park is just on the other side of the lake and is well worth a trip, especially during a full moon, when one can see the very rare phenomena of moon bow on clear nights.

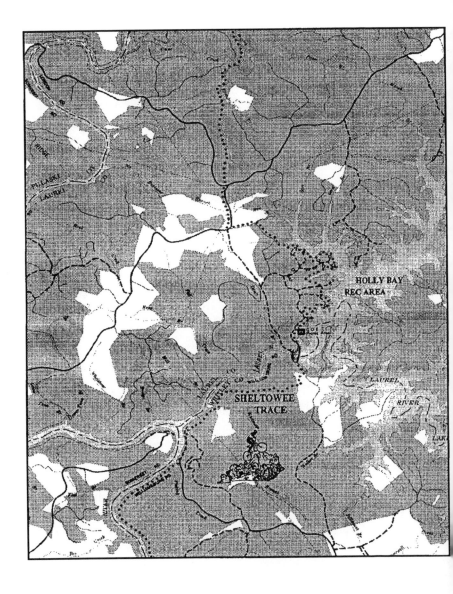

Western Kentucky

The terrain of western Kentucky is sometimes pretty flat and therefore not well known for it's mountain biking potential. The good people at the Purchase Area Mountain Bike Association (PAMBA) are working hard to change that perception.

Based in Paducah, Kentucky, PAMBA is involved in the development of bicycle trails in Land Between the Lakes and the Pennyrile State Park near Hopkinsville. So far, they have secured access for about 20 miles of nice singletrack at LBL and are working with officials at Pennyrile to create a viable trail system there. They also host several bike festivals at LBL, in conjunction with the local road riding club, Chain Reaction.

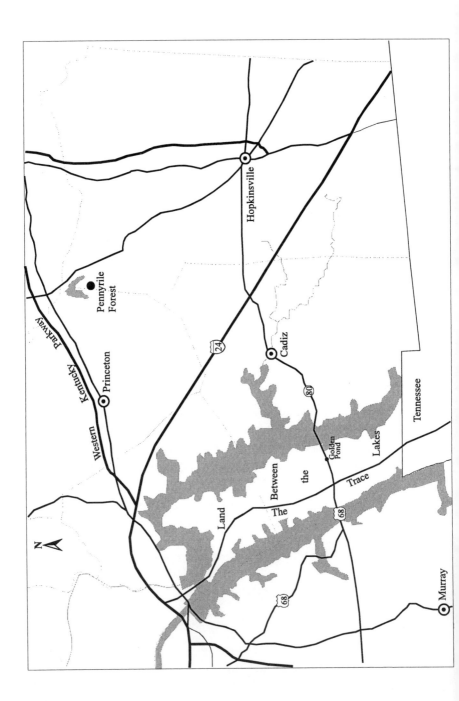

Land Between the Lakes

Rating: Moderate.

Trails: About 20 miles.

Overview: Two main sections comprise this area of narrow, rolling singletrack that drains well and is slightly rocky.

Getting There: Take the Western Kentucky Parkway, West. At I-24, go West (or North, as the case may be) again. Exit # 31, follow The Trace, South to Highway 68, and the Headquarters near Golden Pond. The North South trailhead crosses nearby.

Trail Description: There are two sections currently open to bikes, the first is Golden Pond to Sugar Bay, an out and back of about 12 miles each way and the second is the Energy Lake loop, which is a really well groomed loop around the lake that is partially gravel.

Most trails in LBL are narrow but fast singletrack with sandy soil and small rocks and up to grapefruit sized boulders which are buried in the trail. The terrain is not mountainous but surprisingly rolling with climbable hills of around 100 vertical feet. The relative ease of the riding at LBL is made up for in distance and variety, and there are some technically demanding sections of the Golden Pond to Sugar Bay ride.

Notes: The Park Service is considering opening up more or even all of the 64 mile long North South Trail, of which the Sugar Bay to Golden Pond ride is but one section. Last year the entire North South Trail was open for a special ride organized by PAMBA. Participants rode the entire 64 mile length in two days and reported generally excellent trail conditions throughout.

The land managers at Land Between the Lakes are using a unique criteria for determining whether to open up sections of trail: the amount of use by mountain bikes will be determinative of future openings, in other words the more the area is used by bikers, the more trail the rangers will open up! Financial considerations are paramount in Land Between the Lakes administrative decisions (trail access) since the parks service is being forced to cut back services due to lack of money.

Bugs and especially ticks can be a problem anywhere in the woodlands of Kentucky, but the tick problem seems a little worse at LBL. Bring lots of repellent and don't go into the high grass if it can be avoided. The folks at PAMBA will be able to tell you what is open when you come, also, any numbered road, paved or not, is open to bikes in Land Between the Lakes.

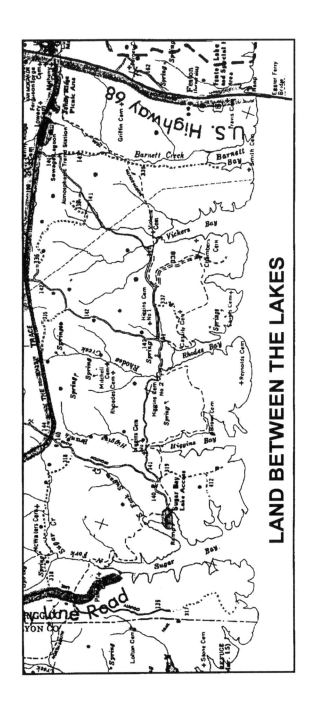

Pennyrile State Park

Rating: Moderate.

Trails: Unknown Distance.

Overview: With rolling terrain similar to Land Between the Lakes, Pennyrile has a lot of potential for excellent mountain biking. It was the first state park to allow biking in Kentucky. Unfortunately, there are no known trail maps. A call to Bikes and More, 502-885-0613, in nearby Hopkinsville may provide more information.

Getting There: Take the Western Kentucky Parkway to Dawson Springs exit, Road 109. Follow signs to main entrance of the park. Follow the park entrance road to the first Y and take a Right. Most rides begin at the fire tower next to the road.

Notes: The Singletrack is similar to Land Between the Lakes with a somewhat rocky, well drained trail.

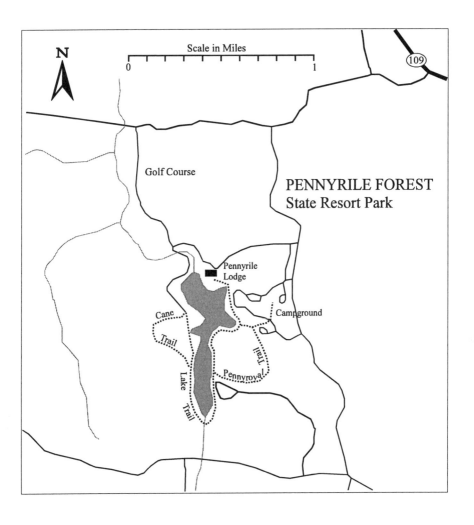

Southern / South Eastern Kentucky

One day the most famous off road bicycling trails in Kentucky will be in the steep hills of southeastern Kentucky, where topography and climate make for superb riding. Southeastern Kentucky is arguably the most remote part of the state which has held back the development of mapped bicycle trails. Even so, the region is replete with opportunity and the various land managements are welcoming bikers with open arms.

Look for trail systems in land held by coal mining companies to open up in the next few years. These companies recognize the public relations benefits that unobtrusive recreation on their land provides. They are actively encouraging local groups such as the Twelfth Mountain, Southeastern Kentucky Mountain Bike Association, to help create trail networks.

Red Bird Purchase is another area which will soon open to bicycles. Unfortunately, development in these areas is too preliminary to be included in any detail. Call the Twelfth Gear bicycle shop in Hazard, Kentucky.

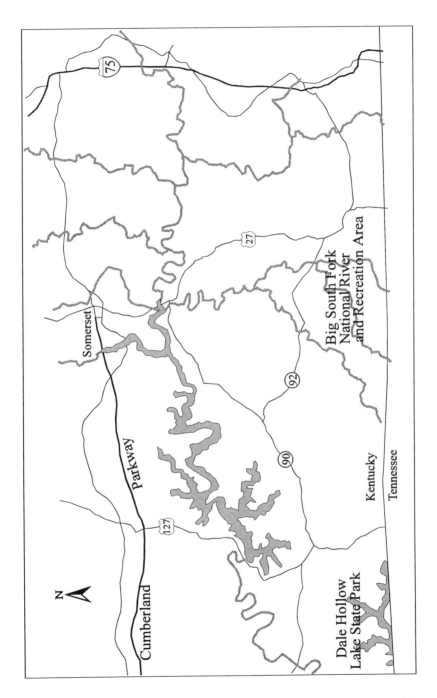

Big South Fork Recreation Area

Rating: Moderate to Advanced.

Trails: Peter's Mountain Loop 12 miles.

Overview: Wide variety of trails and big mountain scenery in an outstanding wilderness environment make this a peerless trail biking destination. This area, which is surrounded by the Daniel Boone National Forest, and bisected by the Sheltowee Trace, is huge, so don't ride there without a map, Big South Fork Recreation Area is on the Tennessee border, so allow for the drive time from northern cities.

Getting There: From I-75 South, take Highway 92, West, at Sterns, Kentucky. Follow signs to Alum Creek Campground.

To access the Tennessee side, and Pickett State Park, take Highway 92, West, to Highway 27, at Pine Knot. Left onto 27, South, to the town of Oneida, Tennessee. Stop at the Oneida outdoor store for the latest information.

Trail Description: Sheltowee Trace crosses the access road to Alum Campground. Take Sheltowee South to Yamacra, staying off spur hiking trails. The trails in the Yahoo Falls area, north of the Alum Campground are off limits to bikes, at least that is what the ranger told us. South of Yamacra, the Sheltowee Trace bears West of the South Fork of the Cumberland River, away from the popular Devils Jump Rapids area. After a few miles, the Trace nears the Tennessee State Line in the shadow of Peter's Mountain, where it meets the John Muir Trail. The Sheltowee Trace goes all the way to Pickett State Park. This would be roughly twenty five miles from Alum Campground, one way.

Peter's Mountain Loop, was recommended by one of the rangers. Take 92 South to Bell's Farm Horsecamp. Turn there. Gravel road leads to top of Peter's Mountain. The trail head begins there. Take the horse trail on the Right, and follow it down to the John Muir Trail. Take a Left on the John Muir Trail as it winds down the mountain. Take the four wheel drive road on the Left, a short ways after crossing No Business Creek, then keep to the up-hill Left trail after crossing Dry Branch (Creek?) for a big push up the side of the mountain. Another Left up the four wheel drive trail, then another Left back toward the car completes this 12 mile loop.

Notes: We have not explored very much of the trail possibilities in this enormous land area. Many trails here were created from old abandoned lumber and fire roads by mountain bikers. The bike and outdoor shop at the crossroads of Oneida, TN will also be able to direct you to the good and open trails.

The bicycle access situation at Big South Fork is not clear. Rangers told some riders we know that the Yahoo Falls area is completely off-limits to bikes, even on the Sheltowee, yet did not seem very concerned when they learned that Yahoo Falls was where these friends had just ridden. A rule of thumb might be to avoid the designated hiking trails except for the John Muir and Sheltowee trails. Horse trails, of which there are many miles at Big South Fork, are generally good and legal to ride upon. But this is just a suggestion. A better idea is to ask a ranger, and while experience has shown us that you may not get a wholly consistent answer from one ranger to the next on the question of legal trails to ride, you can at least be sure that you won't get a ticket!

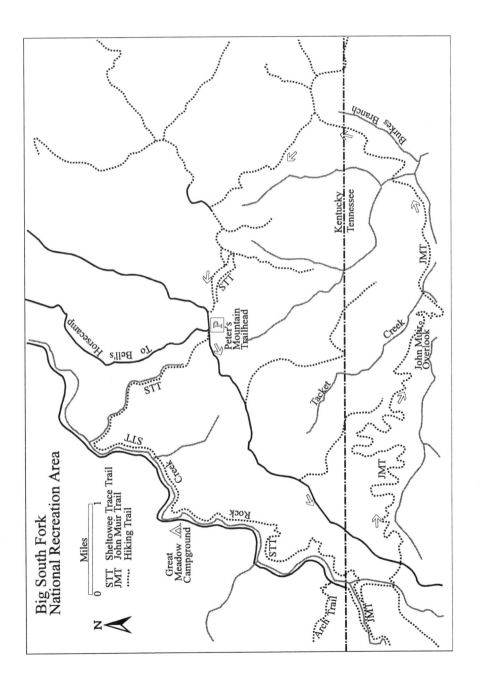

Big South Fork
National Recreation Area

Miles
0   1

STT   Sheltowee Trace Trail
JMT   John Muir Trail
...... Hiking Trail

Great
Meadow
Campground

N

Peter's
Mountain
Trailhead

To Bell's Horsecamp

STT

STT

STT

LLS

Rock Creek

Creek

Tacket

Arch Trail

JMT

JMT

JMT

John Muir
Overlook

Creek

Kentucky
Tennessee

Burkes Branch

Dale Hollow Lake State Park

Rating: Moderate / Advanced 11 miles each way.

Trails: Boom Ridge Trail/Charlie Groce Ridge Trail.

Overview: Dale Hollow is the southernmost and, at over 3000 acres, the second largest state park in Kentucky. Founded in 1971, it is like Big South Fork National Recreation Area in that it shares a border with a park in Tennessee. The dam which created the Dale Hollow reservoir was originally a Corps of Engineers flood control project, but now water borne recreation is the primary focus of the lake which surround the park on three sides. The trails extend atop the ridges, along the entire length of the park and across the state line into Tennessee. The trails are multi-use, which means that meeting horses should be anticipated. Use the usual courtesies and procedures when dealing with these skittish animals. There is a full service campground, but no lodge. The traveler must realize that this is one of the most isolated areas mentioned in this book, and that proper precautions as well as travel time allowances must be taken.

Getting There: From I-75 South, exit at Williamsburg, which is just North of the Tennessee border, as if you were going to the Big South Fork National Recreation Area. Take Highway 92 West, past Big South Fork, to Highway 90, then Left on 90, to Route 449 on the Left. If you get to Burksville on 90, you can access the park by traveling South on Highway 61.

If you are coming from Louisville or the West, take I-65 south to the Cumberland Parkway toll road, then exit on Highway 90 at Glasgow. Take 90 South West to 449.

Look for the signs for Dale Hollow Lake State Park and then signs to State Park Road 6371. Park at the Camp Ground.

Trail description: From the Camp Ground, pick up the Charlie Groce Ridge Trail at section R, following the Groce Trail to it's junction with Boom Ridge Trail. Since the park is on a peninsula, either direction you go on the trail will eventually end at the Dale Hollow Reservoir. The spur trails end at bluffs overlooking the lake. The Boom Ridge Trail is 8 miles, while the entire Charlie Groce Ridge Trail is 3 miles. As you can see from the map, the two trails run together at certain points.

Notes: This is a fairly easy trail but it's length, the rugged terrain, and the isolation of the place merit extra caution and an advanced rating. Look for more trails in the future here and elsewhere, as the less utilized state parks in Kentucky embrace bicycling as a way to attract visitors.

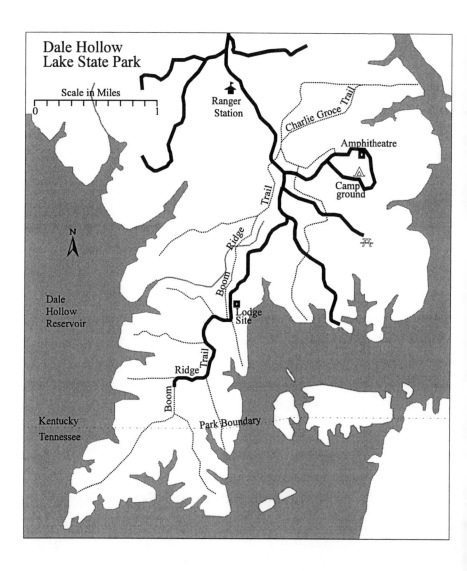

Dale Hollow
Lake State Park

Scale in Miles

0   1

Ranger
Station

Charlie Groce Trail

Amphitheatre

Camp
ground

N

Ridge Trail

Boom

Dale
Hollow
Reservoir

Lodge
Site

Ridge Trail

Boom

Kentucky
Tennessee

Park Boundary

Race Courses

Racing is a big part of off road cycling, where it is as much a social function as competition. Off road races are similar to "fun run" style running races in that the goal of most competitors is personal achievement and riding against the clock.

The atmosphere at races is light and friendly at all but the highest levels of off road racing.

Races in Kentucky are more often than not held to raise money for some trail project or land area. The exception is Bike Butler a for profit race series held in Carrolton, Kentucky, halfway between Louisville and Cincinnati. Races at Butler are big time affairs with racers who travel from hundreds of miles to participate. Nevertheless, the relaxed atmosphere holds true here as well, and Bike Butler races are among the most enjoyable anywhere, for novice or expert.

All of the race courses described here are held on land which is otherwise unavailable for riding, being either private or closed to bicycles. Unfortunately, you will have to wait for the next race in order to ride these excellent trails.

General Butler State Park - Bike Butler

Rating: Beginner to Advanced.

Trails: 5 miles.

Getting There: From I-71, get off at the Carrollton Exit and turn Right. General Butler State Park is on the Left after a short distance. Climb to the top of the hill and turn Right at Ski Butler.

Trail Description: Hand made singletrack snakes around the ski area for a total of five miles. Don't be turned off by the fact that this is a ski slope, most of the trails are in the woods and are high quality. This course is known for its technical difficulty and climbing requirements, over 500 feet of vertical elevation is gained each lap - an Everest like statistic for a Midwestern race course.

Notes: Bike Butler is a ski area during the winter (Ski Butler), which is a growing trend among such resorts looking to extend their season. The five weekend race series is promoted by Richard Mathews, who started with one race in 1989 and has continued to expand the format ever since. The address and phone number of his promotion company is in the appendix at the end of this book, and he will be happy to send you an up to date schedule if requested.

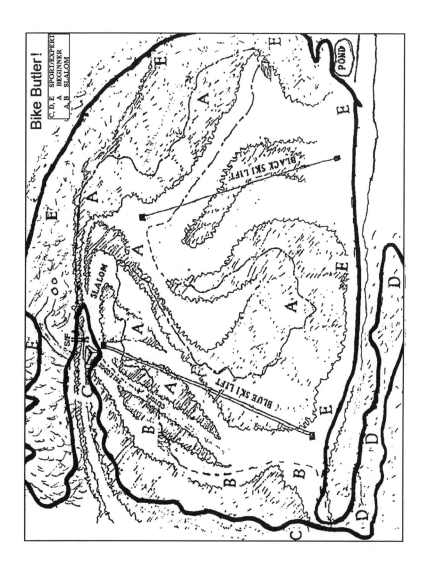

Land Between the Lakes

Rating: Beginner to Advanced.

Trails: 25 miles.

Overview: This course is unique because it is the only traditional point to point race in Kentucky and one of a very few left in the country. Point to point races begin in one place and end in another and require the obvious extra transportation accommodations inherent in this set-up. It is the oldest form of bicycle race, and a direct descendant of steeplechase races on horseback.

Getting There: Most races at Land Between the Lakes are promoted by the Purchase Mountain Bicycle Association and are staged at Golden Pond or Sugar Bay. See the directions for these areas in the description for Land Between the Lakes.

Trail Description: The course at Land Between the Lakes has been described with glowing superlatives by many off road bicycle racers. It is the perfect combination of smooth singletrack and high speed riding that provides a welcome relief from the relentless hills and obstacles of the other race venues. As described it usually consists of a point to point, with racers shuttling to the start area and finishing at one of the major trail beads.

Notes: One of the most fantastic aspects of racing at Land Between the Lakes is that the section of the North - South race course is only open to bikes for special events such as this, and is therefore unknown terrain to the entire field of competition. This situation is such a contrast to the typical race course that sometimes seems all too familiar to the experienced racer.

See map for Land Between the Lakes.

Toil in the Soil - Skylight, Kentucky

Rating: Beginner to Advanced.

Trails: 4 miles.

Overview: The pastoral setting on a horse farm close to Louisville, coupled with some unique terrain and technically demanding singletrack, make this a popular race. The relaxed atmosphere hearkens back to the festival atmosphere which used to distinguish off road from road bike races. Friendliness and camaraderie are the norm, which is a good thing given the difficulty of the course.

Getting There: Skylight is 15 miles East of Louisville on U.S. Highway 42.

Trail Description: The narrow, tree lined singletrack is very challenging with lots of rocks of various sizes cropping up throughout the course. A general lack of big hills moderates the difficulty somewhat, but there are plenty of short steep rises to keep the heart rate up. The technical difficulty, relative flatness and rather short race distances make this course well suited to the huskier power riders.

The premier section "Wicked Ridge" is as challenging as it's name suggests as it snakes around and over huge limestone boulders while traversing the side of a ravine. This section leads to the equally colorfully named trails: "Sinkhole," "Cold Snake," and "Pine Forest Chute." As difficult as these trails may be it is always the hot and bumpy open pasture section which draws the most good natured complaints from the participants.

Notes: This trail is on very private land and is open only for races. The Louisville Chapter of the Kentucky Mountain Bike Association promotes races there about twice a year.

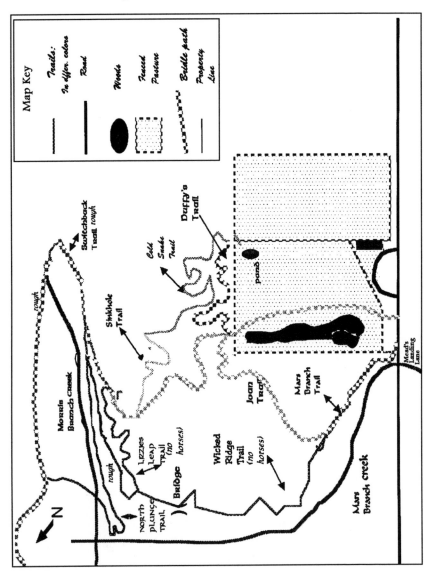

Appendix

Appalachian Mountain Bike Club
Knoxville,Tennessee
615-675-Bike

Big South Fork Bicycle Club
Oneida, TN
615-569-4080

Bike Butler
Richard Mathews
4770 Squiresville Rd.
Owenton, KY 40359-8516
(502) 484-2998

Central Kentucky Cyclists
(Green River State Park Info)
c/o Eddy'O's Bike Shop
502-789-4330

Dale Hollow State Park
6371 State Park Road
Bow, Kentucky 42714
502-433-7431

IMBA (International Mountain Bike Association)
P.O. Box 7578
Boulder, Colorado 80306-7578
303/545-9011
Fax: 303/545-9026

Kentucky Mountain Bike Association
P.O. Box 5433
Louisville, KY 40255-0433
502-569-7676

Northern Kentucky Mountain Bike Association
30 East Southgate Avenue
Fort Thomas, Kentucky 41075

Land Between the Lakes
Tennessee Valley Authority
100 Van Morgan Drive
Golden Pond, Kentucky 42211
502-924-5602

PAMBA (Purchase Area Mountain Bike Association)
c/o Bikeworld
848 Joe Clifton Drive
Paducah, Kentucky 42001
(502) 442-0751
E-Mail: RTS CASH@AOL.COM

Redbird Purchase (66 mi. crest trail)
Daniel Boone National Forest
HC 68, Box 65
Big Creek Kentucky 40914
District Ranger: Dennis Daniels
(606) 598-2192

South East Kentucky Mountain Bike Association:
12th Gear Bike Shop:
Hazard, Kentucky
Paul Woods: (606) 436-6180

About the Authors

Stuart Ulferts, age 31, is an Attorney in LaGrange, Kentucky. He was introduced to bicycles in 1967 when his father began riding one of the first English 10 speeds to be sold in the area. An avid off road cyclist since 1987 when he returned to Louisville to attend Law School, he is also active in the struggle for land access for trail bicycles, and is current president of the Kentucky Mountain Bike Association. Stuart lives with his wife Duffy and four dogs in Louisville.

Bruce Montana, age 45, is a boiler inspector living in Louisville. One of the first off road cyclists in Louisville, He has been instrumental in the establishment of the Metro-area trail network that is maintained by the Kentucky Mountain Bike Association. Bruce is in charge of map making for the club which he was president of for three years. In his small amount of spare time, Bruce makes high quality beer in his home. Bruce lives with his wife Amy, and two children Heather and Neil.

INDEX

B

C

D

F

G

I

J

S

Seneca Park   19
Sheltowee Trace   77, 79, 81, 83, 85
Sheltowee, North of the Dam 62
Star Gap Arch Trail   74

T

Toil in the Soil   111
Turkey Foot to Arvel Section 80

W

Waverly Park 22
West Point   33

Z

Zachariah ATV trails 68
Zilpo / Pioneer Weapons Hunti   59